World Hotel

World Hotel

Reetika Vazirani

 COPPER CANYON PRESS

Cover art: By permission of the British Library, "The building of the
palace at Khawarnaq" or 6810 f154v, from the *Khamsa of Nizami,* art
by Kamal-udin Bizhad.

Copper Canyon Press is in residence under the auspices of the Centrum
Foundation at Fort Worden State Park in Port Townsend, Washington.
Centrum sponsors artist residencies, education workshops for Wash-
ington State students and teachers, Blues, Jazz, and Fiddle Tunes
Festivals, classical music performances, and the Port Townsend
Writers' Conference.

LIBRARY OF CONGRESS CATALOGING-IN-PUBLICATION DATA

Vazirani, Reetika.

World hotel / Reetika Vazirani.

  p. cm.

ISBN 1-55659-183-7

1. Title.

PS3572.A985 W67 2002

811'.54— DC21

2002013452

9 8 7 6 5 4 3 2 FIRST PRINTING

COPPER CANYON PRESS

Post Office Box 271

Port Townsend, Washington 98368

www.coppercanyonpress.org

To
My mother Heea Halder

to
Yusef Komunyakaa

and to
Charles Henry Rowell

ACKNOWLEDGMENTS

My thanks to Valerie Brewster, Michael Collier, Rita Dove, Marilyn Hacker, Sam Hamill, Eddy Hirsch, Neltje, Gregory Orr, Carrie Schaffer, Michael Wiegers, Charles Wright, the Henry Hoyns Fund at the University of Virginia, the Virginia Commission for the Arts, the Corporation of Yaddo, and my family.

I am grateful to the editors of the following publications in which some of these poems appeared:

AGNI, Alaska Quarterly Review, Amerasia Journal, The American Voice, The Beacon Best of 1999 (Beacon Press, 1999), *The Beacon Best of* 2001 (Beacon Press, 2001), *Best American Poetry* 2000 (Scribners, 2000), *Brilliant Corners, Callaloo, Colorado Review, Columbia, Crab Orchard Review, International Quarterly, Kenyon Review, The Literary Review, Massachusetts Review, Meridian, The New American Poets: A Bread Loaf Anthology* (University Press of New England, 2000), *New England Review, Nimrod, The Paris Review, Pequod, Ploughshares, Prairie Schooner, Pushcart Prize* XXIV (Pushcart Press, 2000), *Quarterly West, Shenandoah, Smartish Pace, Southern Review, To Stanley Kunitz, with Love from Poet Friends* (Sheep Meadow Press, 2001), *TriQuarterly, Turnings: Writing Women's Transformations, Virginia Quarterly Review, Washington Post Book World, Western Humanities Review,* and *Women's Review of Books.*

Women have no wilderness in them,
They are provident instead,
Content in the tight hot cell of their hearts
To eat dusty bread.

LOUISE BOGAN

Contents

∾

Inventing Maya

❧

It's Me, I'm Not Home

World Hotel

Hollywood and Hydroquinone

She lightened her skin
played Sousa and Joplin
four-four time we sailed
When she didn't speak
our accents seeped
out of British books

to Mrs. Milner's   port de bras
lambswool on our swollen toes
Giselle   The Merry Widow
If we stared
she opened magazines
long limbs and pale eyes

Our nothing she hoarded
lentils   chilies   channa
her mother   a husband's
overdoses back there with the Tang
his last note recanting *you will*
thus our kitchen a shut drum

six shrimp-cocktail glasses of milk
We ate what we didn't grow
and wore our oldest clothes
through grocery stores
with a hush on our lips   don't touch
this is Maryland   a big country

I am your mother   Invent me

3

Inventing Maya

English

Their Army barracks were fun in the jungle
outside Lucknow, wide paths to tan buildings,
and men wore caps with quarter-moon fronts.
Do caps keep the moon from shining in?
What do they think of ours — we have a hundred
names, a hundred phases, and in England
there's just moon, that's all. And think of the quick
words they used — *Hello. Cheers. Thanks very much
old chap.* Little words from a locked
box and twenty-six letters. So few.

I saw folded napkin, fork-knife-spoon,
cloth and glass and gin-water, gin-tonic, gin-soda;
eating places off in squares like beds
at Christ's Church, headstone, footstone, grass
between. Then the General, he said, *Neat,*
and a bearer brought a clear drink on a tray.
The silver cutlery clicked on the plates,
words like a storekeeper's coins. I didn't want
to leave, but at thirteen hundred sharp we filed out
by a hundred olive quarter-moon caps.

The soldiers
made paths through the jungle to let light in,
wore caps to keep it out, and officers
drove at noon while we sat in the shade.
My uncle, a general, said they are great
adventurers, but their own country is an island.

And when I said *island,* it was a mint leaf
on my tongue, an almond slice, a moon
with its thin rays on the windowpane.

Boarding

1. *Mussoorie, Uttar Pradesh*

In the Himalayas, I ran faster than any girl.
I was six, and then ten. In the dining hall,
cream in the milk cups; and mail my father sent,
marshmallows from Connaught Circus,
Chiminlal's notepaper, Cadbury's chocolate.

Everybody shared: we were a British school,
we read verses in Chapel, many of us, even Hindus.
Fathers and mothers left us quick-quick in our bunks
with photos of them; we waved, then invented friends,
starlets in *Film Fare,* the latest beauty queens
from Bombay, Durban, Rome, and London.

The first day, packages rustling, luggage,
the train so loud tracks hissed.
The Army parade stayed to cheer.
Then the mountain soldiers drove us up.

2. *Holidays*

In maths, Geeta's long black plait —
and Helen's blue ribbon, her frizzled braid —
not very tidy even if Hall Matron is strict.

I am busy and you always muss up your hair—
what would your mothers say—
biting your nails and not sitting straight.

We did, but slumped when she passed us,
her gloomy apron and starched dress.
But I knew at holidays when the others

boarded the train, Miss Naraman,
a Christian lady from Kerala, took me
to her bungalow behind Headmaster's…

Maya, my mother is old. Yours is gone.
All god's children take shelter
at Christmas, even on a mountain.
When Jesus was born, it was quiet, like this.

　　3. *The Divorce*

We get measured and weighed in the spring
and fall. All my life running up
the mountain, but on the map it looks
a thumbnail. Mail never comes,
me on tiptoes passing the windowpane.

But I wish I were taller and far from the judge's
robes, and the sari my mother wore.
Goodbye, my dear. Goodbye, Mother.
And it is never like that again, lustrous silk, shaking.

4. Independence

1947

When I am ten, the British quit.
Headmaster says, *The Great*
Mutiny started it. We repeat,
The Great Mutiny of 1857
in our booming voices. Even
Akbar was Great, even Catherine.
We titter over History. His back
turns; we see his pink spotty neck.

Sorry, the British leaving? we beg.
This is hardly a quiz—
sit up, he spits.
It is about trains and ships
you love, city names. As for me,
I'm old. I'll end in a library.
I began in trade. But you must stay,
we tell him. He lived here as we have

but longer. He says he was alive
in Calcutta in 1890. He didn't
have a rich father. He came with
The Tea Company; we saw a statement
on his wall. They built
railroads to take the tea "home
to England" so Darjeeling and Assam
could be sipped by everyone,

us and them. They sold Ceylon —
silk, pepper, sapphires, cotton.
Of course they wanted what we had.
In England there's just wool, salt, snobs, and
foggy weather, Shakespeare. We make a trade.

5. *The Dadar School for the Blind*

They ask me, *What are shadows?*
I don't know. They are dark and
you can't see them. *Oh,*

they say, *do you want to stack dominoes?*
Ved says, *Didi.* Sister.
God, like when I forgot

what sugar was, and *with.*
Tea with sugar. Four o'clock.
The dominoes clatter. I must stick

them back, one with one, six
with six, smooth Kalpana's hair
with almond oil. When Braille is over,

we walk with Ayah or ride
to Malabar Hill, the Parsi Tower
of Silence Vedi asks about.

I say, *I don't know why birds eat
dead bodies in a stone pit.
Don't cry. You didn't die.*

I hit him for pestering me
if dark things get lonely.
What can I say? *Yes go*

stop no. Doormen flag taxis
down for families who
holiday. I am a beggar-girl,

not a principal's daughter.
Get on with it, the judge rushed —
Little girl, who will you live with,

your mother? Father says,
You are good, stay with me.
Who chose? Ved and I

are stick people forever
climbing the brown hill.
My father named me Maya.

What does he know?
I'm lured in this world.
A girl, I have lost my way.

6. *Graduation*

Today I notice how lush it is since I came when doorways seemed large. We planted the holly bushes.

Thin in a white sari, Miss Naraman says, *Maya, I'll be gone when you return. For your first Sunday in America, take this — keep the gold border polished. Don't marry until you finish. Write to me.*

Yes Aunty, thank you Aunty.

In my room, I pack the yellow sari, petticoat, silk for a blouse, and a picture of school — white with red roof tiles, the mountain absolutely green. I won't think of it. Like the recent war, when it ended, we little ones were told.

In a few weeks, Rekha will meet her husband. When they phoned, her parents had already traded beauty for his land.

Friday Mixer

The Chapel Hill Rotary invited me twice,
and I wore Aunty's yellow sari. I laugh;
for ten years I lived on a mountain.
I show them Mussoorie.
They say it looks like the Blue Ridge.
They're fascinated by so much silk —
six yards on me — but I like
skirts, scarves, red nail polish, and
I will have to learn to dance.

Sheila says, *Wear that costume.*
Not a dress?
No, she says.
I say, *You can't quick dance in a sari.*

She hands me her best tea-length dress —
emerald crepe with netting over the skirt.
Then even geography and skin dim
to a few lights in the dance hall,
music blurs into shoes and fabric
five hundred years ago, a masked ball,
given by the Queen of Spain for her friend
the Duchess who sailed days across a flat world.

The Great Hall

At four, we put on our slacks.
Sometimes it's sherry. We are not to drink,
not to mention Professor X.
Margaret, he touched her leg and winked.

There is whispering for Dara, thrill
and envy. Bold ones we admire,
but we do not understand them.
Sometimes two walk off or laugh.

When we ask, they don't tell.
They are lucky, but we don't know
if that is what pearls are.
They make plans and leave,

looking at you. I wait
for Phyllis with her bucket. We stop
at the great portrait of Katherine
Whitehurst, cream chiffon, the sandy coast

of Hatteras. She's holding orchids.
She had no children. Then came this building
and the scholarship, Lady of the Hall,
lilies for Easter, the New Year toast,

a drawn bath and salts, dinner on a tray,
cedar closets, and a mirror to say *Live with me,*
I will always furnish what you knew...
I try on names. Maya Whitehurst.

I forget no one skipping down the stairs,
a man in the foyer cooing, *How do you do?*
I'm colored. I greet myself, and
the ceiling feels like whispering.

Tiffin for Tea, Lorry for Truck

...desiring melancholy like most English people...

VIRGINIA WOOLF

To say he got out of his village by cunning
and hard work — you have heard that story.
But at university, he stepped out, wing

tips to fedora. Indians looked at my father.
Just as the British withdrew, he sided
with Nehru. At forty, he stopped changing.

Twenty years in New York, he still wore
a three-piece suit with a pocket watch.
His vests looked like winter and spring

there's metal in the sky, it might never
rain, or you left your umbrella in the cab.
Fog owns the morning and you can't travel.

Chanel Lipstick

Daddy always said this many
rupees gets a dollar. When I
bought my first lipstick,
it was as if I bought a cow
in India. It was always what
I could have had in Delhi.
On holiday at Reno Road,
he'd hint D.C. was not home.
That's why he didn't want me
window-shopping downtown,
but I went anyway — I took
the bus and walked over
to Woodward & Lothrop,
Lord & Taylor, to the glass
cases of perfumed powder.
They change you — Libreville,
Bombay, Cairo, Caracas;
see them under the careful
light when the assistant tilts
the mirror for your ease.
　　　This summer vacation
I bought my second red
in a lacquered case. Walking,
I hid its darkness on my skin
between me and the city.
The steady rubbing off
brought another color
to my lips. I sailed halfway

round the world wearing
saris and summer shoes,
browsing, spending dollars,
my love for places, taking
one suitcase, my passport
photo lipsticked like this.

The Bus North

When I saw him looking, I held myself in.
He saved me a seat. *Window or aisle?*
Aisle please. Where I sit at the cinema.
He looked at me like a bulbul bird eyeing
warm weather, dark skin, a split papaya.

I was all Hawaiian to him,
I smiled automatically, I don't know why
he gave me his card, asked me for mine;
maybe I liked his height, striped shirt, his grin,
I'm a boutonniere to be pinned.

The bus whirs and your spirit flies
behind a buzz of delays. When he got off
in Richmond I felt a bitter fizzle.
D.C. again, taxi home, the guest room.
Two weeks later a stiff envelope came.

May I drive you back to school
I bought a green Ford convertible
stay Thanksgiving with us in Richmond

   William Stratford

I said, *It's from a Rotarian with questions*
about caste and incarnations…
My father said, *Good, you are capable,*
and we are honoured you see to travel so far.

William's Visit

He came like a slipknot   his car
a dot beyond the plaza of cafés where
we sat   Pennsylvania Avenue a coffee
shop at G Street my-name-is don'tleaveme
a two-week visa give me four   I felt
about Paris the way I felt about him

what he would do to me six feet tall
eyes grinning white skin I am not
from here but what I'd give
I'm nineteen years terrible I'll-tell-
you-everything-in-an-hour
and I'm left churning *if I were*

but I kept hearing us laugh *were*
white as I dreamt we would past the District
Building sun setting balmy before rain
we wandered towards his car   I mentioned
the weather *why not take my arm till dark*
pretend it's Paris June light until eleven o'clock

May Queen

YOU'RE PRETTY said the sign
Am I?
I voted for another
lost by one vote
Tiaras are for
a Mary

I hold her train
smooth her hair
the spotlight struck her nape
looked even lighter that night
I eased myself in the tub
porcelain

holding white heat
I ask for the moon I do
Others get it I slip
Mother may I?
No you may not
take this turn to be loved

Nudes

Manet Degas   in a book
Pissarro   speck
upon speck   water lilies nude
bathers   a breast
gloves at the opera
couples abandoning ship
wooing *Child don't cry*
we'll be back at sunup

Next day the sun a dot
to map my bearings
My cabin's near the dark
Stevedores hauling my trunk
aboard   the door says WHITES ONLY
Who am I in the middle of?
Puffs of steam quickly the train took me
from a black umbrella on the street
My gaze is holding
Berthe Morisot's slender fingers
on a sofa taking one lover
to X out a gentleman

Who will paint the bad blood between us?
In their time peonies and zinnias became cinema
I see my mother point to pleasure
like an unplucked root   Father your money
was a cold smile and the British
I started to talk like them

My camera forgave no one
My album   my atlas
Bombay London New York
father mother three of us
nude room I'm in the middle of

It's Raining

after Vicente Aleixandre

For so long there is nothing to do.
Maryellen knocks and says, *Maya do you want to walk?*
But I only listen and hope for something better.
Everyone returns. Also it is Sunday,
like childhood before bed, no lights anywhere except outside.
Even books get limp. I cross the long slow gap, one word to
          the next.
Our mascot Brandy, his snout buried under a paw.
I find Maryellen needlepointing, and she asks if I will go,
even in the dark. *Yes,* I say, *let's go.*
She is more generous than I and puts her sewing down.
So we wear slickers and boots and walk arm in arm into the rain,
past the brick halls, the white gymnasium, and the oblong dome,
right down the dark shiny street past wet auto lots.
With no plan, we pass traffic lights
and say something about walking
till Monday when the dorm monitors change,
because we want to break rules.
The council will fine us.
The sound rises like drums, water slips from our yellow coats,
a thin yellow glow surrounds us:
we are bright, two bulbs nearing the city from a dark roof.

What I Was Thinking When He Didn't Write

Helen lives in Germany
Rekha with twins in Jaipur
I never wrote back
      Will Aunty's letter come?
Headmaster Withers condolences
as if a reunion could

Novels find endings
I have my address book thumbed through
my loosening plait
shaken out each evening
and envelopes so light
      Did I miss your birthday?

Seems like I fall
      What's the time zone?
Sheets pushed down I wake up in winter's cold
My body what unrelief to always clone myself
All I had and all I knew is thinning into a squint
and my love is punishing me with his hard wind

What My Best Friend Said to Console Me

Neera says The tall Virginian
drove so far
to see you last summer for a day
and that is a win
his green Ford car top down you're smiling
in heaven at twenty
Catch the American
you have two years I have one

To Richmond and Back

We hope after William marries
he'll honeymoon in the Indies
on a lark his mother said   my wrist
like dark teak I looked at
the ball and claw feet on the mean
table   how did they get there?

William drove me back
the radio went on
songs and ads for biscuits
sharp air   my heels caught
leaves up to the dorm
we said bye the way a plane

shoots across like hope
then nothing   days later
I found a letter   an Indian
in New York to give a talk in
three months at Chapel Hill I saw
a two-karat ruby in prongs

My Brother, the Wedding

Daddy walks me slowly past the guests and they rise
moving aisle after aisle like heat on macadam.
I don't recognize anyone
I sat with in class for sixteen years,

moving aisle after aisle, heat on macadam.
I see flowers, stained glass, the crucifix
I sat with in class for sixteen years,
and you in a sailor suit,

rings on a cushion, spit-shined shoes,
only six years, and fifteen between us.
Did I know you my summers home?
Your paper boats not still for a minute.

I could leave with the groom. A photo,
that's marriage. Paper bows, silver,
one minute two say I do,
in seconds you see them waving.

You leave the groom. That's marriage.
Goodbye brother, save your coins for a trip.
Two say I do in seconds, you see them waving.
Wish for me, I wish for you, ship's in, we have to run.

Daddy walks me slowly past the guests
and they rise, wishing for me,
I for you. Ship's in.
I don't recognize anyone.

Going to See the Taj Mahal

When we set out on the train to Agra
I thought, What an old palace we are going to see,
it's a mausoleum, sixteen fifty-three;
I was tired, and you hired a taxi.
You couldn't even wait, white marble, black stone
tracery, Koran verses against moonlight you said.
And there beyond our driver's wheel I saw
the large dome and four surrounding.
The lightness stood out so clearly for a moment
I forgot this (the long stretch of grass leading up):
the Empress Mumtaz, she bore fourteen heirs.

But what did I know of her except this tomb?
So I pictured her not a beauty, nor especially devout,
always slow to cover her head.
On Thursdays when the open market came
past the red stone quarry, she dressed as her handmaid
and took a poor cloth sack into town where she bartered
for beads women wore on working days; and secretly
with cheap dyes she'd paint herself into the wild casual
beauty of youth, kohl inexpertly applied but alluring.
Then she gave her sack away or left it on the road
should someone find it hoarded in her suite —
the Empress buying this five-and-dime glitter.
And she could see her life without the royal curfew,
places she couldn't go — daily attractions at the well
too scandalous to name.

If only the Emperor's architects knew her,
to free them from this grave,
to free them from the so-called glamour of a Mumtaz.

Maharaja of Patiala

The fancy dress I wore was the wrong one.
They saw me for what I wasn't; I didn't disabuse them,
so I was lost.

ALVARO DE CAMPOS (FERNANDO PESSOA)

I

The Palace opened Sesame.
Our Maharaja tall and handsome.
        Come, he took us in.
His daughters Daisy and Mina offered to show me.
Kiran said, *Maya you haven't seen a lotus in so many*—
Time flew, the men stayed put, and I skipped out with the girls.

Quadrants of clipped hedges and watered roses.
The central fountain teemed with lotus,
        a few jewel-green frogs,
a croquet lawn to mirror English gentry.
We were what was left of it
and thin men bending to keep us.

The girls kept asking about men
and America. Their father said,
Don't be greedy for the world.
You're twenty-one, they chimed,
        You married Daddy's doctor.
It hadn't occurred to me I said yes to things.

2

At four, we ate sweets overlaid with silver,
a sheet of hope on a bright lake we couldn't see.
Among brambles, we romped, impatient
       for a man's reflection.
The wicked godmother of hearts
digging into our petticoats with her spade.

Girls rushing
to swallow the locked palace.
       Cities — to go.
But I couldn't warn them —
they'd see it themselves —
you outgrow a father and then what?

Long June days in Paris. I saw Versailles —
       a throne, a mirror, an urn.
In his bedroom, godmother let it happen.
Father-free, mother-haunted, I said goodbye.
I married a man.
I thought I'd dance through open doors.

3

Our house was ready. We mixed
with the washerman and egg-collector.
I travelled out with Kiran, but I wanted
a big house, that tall white
       man from Virginia,
me on that bus, a Chanel suit

striding through my mother.
In the villages bright-eyed children
greeted me like a queen;
from the backs of clay houses
        came garlands I bowed into.
Marigolds, limber arms.

For an instant I smiled — my legs
forever brown of a people, brown
        of a source. Was it?
It had always been the tang
of khaki on my tongue: I said
my children.

Pergola

Let me tell you about roses climbing
along columns in the Rani's garden;
I have walked it, top terrace
spanning eighty-two paces: the sand
would get absolutely printed,
until the gardener comes with his rake,
but others file in. The sand begins to look
like roses, bushes of every kind,
even Spanish roses which
recalled the Alhambra to the Queen.
She spoke fondly of Spaniards steering
galleons of gold—and of Moguls
bringing minarets to Spain,
just as she sent her envoy first-class
to bring her roses from abroad.
But what do I know of the Alhambra?
The heavy fragrance around the Palace,
the Rani who stayed put, sending men out
to bring her variety, the pergola,
roses you've read too much about.

One Week in the Village

Patiala, Punjab

Come, my beloved, let us go forth
into the fields, let us lodge in the villages.

SONG OF SOLOMON 7:11

But he saw my lost look
near other women bathing
sari tucked between my legs
both of us nearing
the daytime rattle of copper
vessels   debates about the cost
of fish and the loud
voices of those who had
no books to brace
them in the havoc

Western-Trained in the Other World

He bolted out of bed full of ideas.
Bathed and groomed he snapped at his chauffeur.
At the Clinic he hammered at his desk—
patents pending if there were time to file.
He dashed off case studies—abscesses on
the child's wan cheeks. He drained them.
A year later the child died of malnutrition,
and the mother paid the bill with eggs and roti.

What a village! He dreamt up an autoclave
and vast greenhouses on the lazy gods' lips.
He was a minnow in the tank of Asia.
He wished for less dust on roads where crops smelled
like the cash of forgetting, and you led your wife in
a fox-trot, saw yourself in black tuxedos.

Aerogram Punjab

We sailed by Africa, back home.
You're good with maps; to find me
first find you in your atlas, your page,

not a tropic, a dashed line —
where did the whale go? Find
the page black. *Chota bhai,* tell me

where the world goes. Are you sledding
to the Lincoln Memorial, brother, tell me.
You're seven. Can you read *New Delhi?*

Say hello to Daddy for me. The tailor
made you a red kemize. Nude, every
day my stomach grows. What else —

sari never changes its size; our tailor's
discount. I have grown. What ails
me? Maybe it's a girl, my dowry-

free holiday. I'm a globe.
Some say a boy. I doubt it —
she moves like the ocean,

and the globe feels tighter.
Sail to Africa, to India.
She's not Asian.
You're good with maps. Find me.

Gina Lollobrigida

She struck all of us city brides.
We didn't discuss what she had, what we wanted
more than magazine covers haunted
our closets; news of her and men with whom
she was seen, "The Woman of Rome."

Her lipstick brought us to darken our own.
Her brow arched slightly more over her left eye.
This too we copied as if our century called for Cleopatras.
We drew brows in black kohl, wore black bras
and perfume. We dressed in petticoats, then saris.

We did not understand what clothes made
us lose. Flawless but not-too, we just copied
her secrets at face value. We tinted
our lips and practiced the dare to be taken.

Rahim Multani

How can a woman resolve
her marriage, save by lies? I have not learned
from others. I speak of my own life. She
stays at home, the man goes forth. A husband's
        absence, a daughter's
        anger, a lover's
suspicion — that is her lot.

RICHARD HOWARD

1. *King Prawns*

When Kiran went out of town I took the girls to get haircuts in Delhi. It wasn't often I could get there. But I wasn't the youngest bride anymore, and I could be seen out with his friends.

Hard liquor, parties, everyone had been to London, Hong Kong, New York; you could smell the foreign currency in the smiles — cold peppermint, white nickel, then the warm gold around our necks like foil. *She's a beauty. She I envy. He's minting money. He's a prince and always will be. And how is Lokhun? Long time we have not seen Amrita.*

That's the way it went at night, sip, sip, we smiled between the facts we traded, the lies we harboured, or the truths we harboured and the lies we spread like cheer. Who's earning what and who we would slander. We all had money, drivers, got haircuts at Connaught, bought Swiss chocolates, and these nights we wore our best saris, women everywhere rustling in the room.

41

2. A Dropped Shawl

There he was, Rahim, owner of the Delhi Palace Grand, in raw silk, Nehru jacket and trousers; Kiran's cousin, not a cousin, but a neighbor in the Bombay refugee camp. He'd made his family's money again; he had backers. And he charmed me with a headwaiter's fastidious air. He told me things about Kiran I never knew, courage during the Hindu-Muslim protests of the forties. And British Quit India. Kiran would fight, hell with Gandhi's salt march.

Then Rahim told me to stop, to come by myself and stay a week.

From the back of a bookshelf he got a flask of scotch. I wore a wool blouse and shawl. The main room buzzed with chatter. Rahim pressed closer, *Remove your shawl, the room is heated.* It was and so I did. I felt like the beach at Malpai clear of the broad palms, a stretch of sand to sweep your eyes over. Then I knew everything. A dropped shawl led to a dropped jacket, his breath the heat of a hand; it is just what I wanted. Kiran, he was on a plane over London. Rahim was his cousin; not his cousin, but a brother from the camp; not a brother, his best friend.

3. If Only a Taste

A car came from the Delhi Grand
I packed my bag and took the train home
His voice trailed   *Drop your bag and come to me*
What he wanted I wanted

Me all my life I said yes because you wanted me to
but this time I meant it

Did I mean it? I did
Would I again? I would
I think of the hotel
the cool stroke he left on my shoulder when he took off my shawl
He poured me a scotch
His look asked would you and I said I would

4. *A Husband's Return*

I was expecting rain for a week no rain came
Like a heavy period waiting for the blood to drop
Kiran's car pulled in I found myself
wearing a smile I could not fathom Rahim
he quickly burnt away like morning
mist a stick of wheat blown off a—

a catch in the mouth Kiran kissed
me absently a landlord on his land
a warrior with no rivals
I felt dutiful and guilty sealed and
unconcealed my skin
held Rahim's scent and nothing else

Daughters in the Morning

When Kiran and I left in the evening
I gave each girl a coated mint
they thought a silver bead
Two girls holding Ayah's hand
and we drove off to a party

Two of them brought morning
dotting over the floor
through the wicker chairs   Had it
rained?   Tara looked out the door
like my mother buying a basket
from the head of a woman   The wicker
scattered light under the table legs
a vase of flowers on the bed
in disarray   windows strewn
across the floor and the jute mats
uncooked rice shimmering in pieces

You came to me children my jewelry
lovely to be here my body made
what we had in the morning
wide sheets   that was
the bright lake my darlings

The Lover

Odd this hotel privacy. Married
but living as I had in the States —
dorm girl in her room.
I took the train from Patiala,
left the girls with Ayah, and lied,
I'm with Faye and Daisy.
Had to say what he'd approve of.
Go then, Kiran said, crushing large rupees in my hand.

Have I been here a week? I've slept
so long I can't remember who was
with me last night in bed, that figure
leaning against the door?
Did he leave me this gold bangle?
I can feel its heft around my wrist, knobs
and crests, a design from the high
Mogul period of Aurangzeb.

I have come to Delhi
to remember our ancient past — so little, a bangle,
what else?
When it slid over my hand,
I opened myself like a book and you hear
its private pulsing. In the quiet he said,
Put your hand here to save your place.
I put my hand there, and he pressed it.
He sat with me a minute, he went away,
left something to hinge me in the wind of myself.

Empire is large land and I can't touch it.
A smile is a root my mother said don't bother.
I am dark. I am small. I married a dark talent
from a small world. The parent who.
The British voices who.
I became those who bent me.
I am dark and small.
Until he asked me to drop my shawl and slid his finger
on my shoulder, let me taste our leisure.
It required my defiance of the small world.
He asked would you, and I said I would.
I read him. I drank up history and peeled back glossy lies.
I had harped on grandeur,
but the Taj Mahal and Rome are a fantasy.
What's left is my darkness.

For so many years I kept my mantra:
They are great and I am small.
I disowned myself as some have by leaving.
I've slept. I've tasted my own milk.
I feel a circle on my wrist.
I'll raise my girls, then I'll be back.
If I never sip this again, I already tasted the morning.

Dream of the Evil Servant

1

We kept war in the kitchen.
A set of ten bone china plates, now eight.
As if a perfumed guest stole her riches…

The next day she wanted to leave at noon.
I said, *Be back by four, I'm paying you.*
She sat by the door,
she put out her hand,
her knuckles knocked against mine,
hard deliberate knuckles. I gave her cash.
Off to watch movies, off to smoke ganja.

2

She came back late and high as if my fear asked for it.
I called her *junglee.*
Everything went off late —
dinner, the children getting into bed;
but the guests understood:
they had servants too.

She stuck diaper pins in my children.
I cursed her openly. Who shouted?
Or I cursed her silently and went my way.
She stole bangles my husband's mother bought,

47

bangles a hundred years old. But she wore frayed jewelry
hawked on the street. She was like a rock that nicked
furniture in corners you'd think only a rat could go.

3

Why didn't I dismiss her?
I don't know.
She got old as I got old.
I could see her sharp shoulder bones
tighten, her knuckled skull.
I had to look at her. It had to wound me.
Listen, said my mother. *Yes mother,* I listened, crouched in my head.

Looking over the flowered verandah she said:
Who are you to think you are beautiful?
What have you got to show?
Go sit on your rag.
All my life I tended to looks,
they betrayed me. I bore you.
I am wretched. Be my mother. Be my maid.

Pandavas' Gamble

> Our country is closed in, all mountains
> that have the low sky as their roof day and night.
>
> GEORGE SEFERIS

Returning from the Capitol
he told me the Ministers focus
on farms not institutes
not hospitals   My bangles rattled
Nothing for the cities   for those
who studied abroad nowhere to go

He froze when Hari asked *Did Sahib*
want his shoes reshined? Want
more breeze   a glass of water?

He looked up the road   no postman
no tailor no sellers with carts I took
off my jewelry for the night like a game
of dice he went up to the gate
To go now meant take nothing

A Night on the *Queen Mary*

Counting heads to New York,
steamer trunks, a few light bags
with my four children.
Another ship trumpets by us.
Husband, what's the harm
if we leave the Christmas lights on?
I call the neighbors to visit;
who's missing? Four breaths warm.

Tick-tock, what a bed to count sheep in,
I drank so much coffee today.
I'm thirty, left my wedding gifts
in Punjab, Kiran will get his visa later.
Friends saw me off at the dock.
We'll meet again trading garlands
at Victoria, our Queen Mother's
Terminus, under the clock.

Porters, luggage,
Miss Naraman, housemother peeking
in she almost stops, and in the corridor
I find others wandering around in robes.
I'm a compass, we skirt the globe,
it's too early for the morning star
in the west, night walking the deck—
I follow this narrow passage

at Rajendra Hospital. I gave birth.
Twelve houses slept in,
aeroplane, train, Greyhound—
the walk from Union Station
to taxi in the rain. The year
runs on hope, buoys you up.
In the best year a light suitcase.
Did I have one

watching Le Corbusier build Chandigarh
rising by the wheat fields?
Or at Malpe, we swam, or cocktail
parties? What year licks the Queen's
face to postcards? Everyone I knew
lived abroad, and in those days airmail
was my hinge, whizzing.
To get that man I got busy—

pregnancy riveted me, I felt thrilled
across the ocean, black page
of the wind lets loose, the speed
of metal cutting into waves,
your blown wishes snag the salt.
Moving, all I've ever wanted
is cupboards filled and
the glamour of a certain age.

Light on the waves' wedges
opens the children's eyes—
pillows, windows, berth;
their big feet next to zip bags—
for me too little room to pack in.

We're all dressed and go upstairs.
They walk like tall sailors
in white uniforms and white caps,

Australian voices mapping life
back home — they've trailed continents,
crew rides free. *The whole trip*
and not a bit's mine unless it all is,
one says. He'd like to take his children
packs of ten-pound notes, for a roof.
Travel, hearing lives on the other side and
your own voice picks up someone else's.

Gardening: Hollywood Lane

To buy peat, dung, it was crazy.
I started from clippings as neighbors did—
coleus took, magenta and its greed,
from a sprig to a load,

leaves like tie-dye next to the talcum
of dusty miller, and the azaleas
in front. Mums bloom
in lieu of dahlias

by the charcoal grill
in Punjab. Jean brought dozens
of periwinkle shoots for the hill,
I gave her phlox, we went on

trading, her children slept overnight,
we swapped outgrown football jerseys.
Beneath the spigot in the back, mint
and coriander for Thursday's chutney.

Limber but too-thick forsythia out by
the shed. In two years rampant
yellow bursts, you could see
the pollen. As for the hanging baskets

along the carport beams, I pictured
petunias every year.
To Deirdre I hinted perennials.
The pots stayed empty, until summer

at one of the children's birthday parties
she brought an armload up — purple
and green vines, wandering Jew she'd
rooted on her windowsill.

Ramayana

You cabled *Tomorrow I am coming*
Bombay to Montreal
The eighteen months fit in an envelope
a mail slot   no sleep

Lipstick I saved for weddings and births
the girls in pleated skirts
and white blouses   our son in a sailor suit
my father driving us to the gate

No it was only my best afternoon sari
purple with patterns of horses
bandani mosaic   eyes in the cloth
kept me warm as distance
froze between the moon and me

Watching the News

Once I was beautiful...
That's how it goes with us.

FRANÇOIS VILLON

There wasn't a rifle at my head,
things did not happen at knifepoint.
Now I recall how I dotted a map,
connected cities, saw Palestine,
blue background with white city dots,
magnification of blocks where the killing was,
then the footage, stores and storekeepers,
I see streets I lived on, where Grand
Union stood, Sheila, Mary Jo, Irene:
Leonard Avenue, Rosemary Hills.
And I see tall fronds of the tropics,
the way it could have been for me
but never was, some other man to marry,
and a good wind.

But who lets the day slide in a greasy pan?
Sunday's roast beef, potatoes, green beans.

The film clips of people waiting
for the prisoner, no letters for eight years.
I know waiting is Bombay to France,
husband over there, me here.
I crossed to and back again.
Then don't come you don't know me I can't say who I

I'd cook dinner, sometimes,
I'd go outside. A driver
thought his wife vanished,
she had lost her memory
in Alabama, called at last collect.
The thrill of being without her, who am I,

is it already morning? Two commutes,
then dinner. Your address changes twice.
The slant of your best friend's face —
she painted jacks in 1945.
I am too young to know the war,
only the way rain ripples the metal roof
of the science shed from the time before
Sir Edmund Hillary,
as if I were with him on that snow. Our father.

Sometimes I watch the six o'clock news
again at ten, Riyadh, Raleigh, all of Spain,
or I'm out in Colorado — breath
of a blue god, blue brow of a nation,
and brown terrain welcoming as moccasins.

Beads on a Mala

...tired Maya going to my maker
the children please look after them
He left upended bottles
of Valium in a scented temple
to an incarnate lord I phoned
the paramedics I phoned the dean

Downstairs little ones with the police
Me I'm with my devil
the mother everyone leaves
I am stuck in the world
When Kiran leaned on me I let him
suffer my fractions I'd gotten that mean

Out back I pulled weeds all day
I lack the salt of the earth   God
what was the point of it
hours a day plucking stray hair
standing at the vanity
where I bleach me

Quiet Death in a Red Closet

Fourteen anniversaries.
Thirteen moons,
A baker's dozen.
Eleven moves.
Ten attempts.
Nine lives.
Eight spoons.
Seven of us.
Six survive.
Five children.
Four daughters.
Three stay.
Too far away.
In marriage,
Someone had to go.

Maya to Herself and Then to Her Gardener

Grass cut trees need pruning
I was unsure of myself   Hence this garden
World I did wallow
envied my daughters my son loyal no
matter what my spurned self ruined

my bones' lack of milk
I still binge on coffee to wake me up cocktails
to put me down   Mack come in
For years we puttered over pachysandra
Have I paid you?

Why do you never pocket my tip?
So   you were always like me
guided by the paranoia that lurks near love
No it's not too early I
already made coffee have some I am up

Letter to Jaipur

...the shallows smell like closets full of last
summer's clothes.

BORIS PASTERNAK

I wanted to tell you
about those years I sat with the children
in the kitchen teaching them to eat.

I wanted to phone you in Jaipur
with your own Ranjit and Ambika,
when the house filled up beyond belief—

the closets with the children's things,
the pantry emptying and filling.
I wanted to tell you, Rekha,

I made mistakes. I didn't fret
as when we were young.
I went on with the spot on the wall,

sink half-full, clothes
I wouldn't fold. Every day
I'll say there was joy,

but it was never what we had in mind
looking into a hand mirror,
sunning in the glass-encased drawing room

we called Our Place. The mountain flowers'
steep slope down
where we stickered our passports

for Switzerland and Russia.
Czarinas perfumed in the snow, scarves,
cousin-sisters, friends.

I wanted to tell you
before I send you my daughters
this summer — next time send yours —

Rekha, teach them the distance
between us is tiny — you see it
when the light pours into a room

dusted before the day rose.
Geography is airmail paper, that's all,
lint slanting in the sun's column.

Days in Punjab

The sansevieria plants were vicious and hardy along the bricks
  in front.
And when relatives visited, my mother-in-law's tongue was
  quick to the point.

In the dining room, lotus floated in a bowl; and when they
  wilted, we took our time removing them.
Every day I contended with dust on the window and over six
  yards of my sari's hem.

And of the banyan tree, I'd think abundant: the peepal and
  palmyra grew wild beyond our garden.
Pantry left unlocked, the servants stole food I'd later need, though
  I took it and even them for granted.

Mali watered the lawn morning and night and reported on
  rosebushes: *blooming, Memsahib.*
For shopping, Faye and I travelled by train to Delhi until the
  curfew kept us in Punjab.

Fervid, the patch of mint never failed me. I'd shred some in jugs
  of water.
My son dug a ditch between raids and lined the gap with cloth
  should any cat need shelter.

Those evenings we debated how we would improve the country
  in some way.
We grew fruit trees, never short of guavas in season; I see they
  were lovely.

We threw kitchen scraps and old flowers to the eager goats at the
    back door.
At three, we waited for the postman's cycle bell and had tea a
    few times before the war.

Seeta

Packing is an India's women's,
I wonder every time how I manage it
& I have done it thirty-four times, by count.

JOHN BERRYMAN

Thinking myself between cities,
histories I could have lived,
the fourteen houses, a long walk
when the tonga driver stopped to speak.
Joy at an airport lunch,
and on a cycle I pedalled off
searching and ending a search.

My life was not always a husband,
the daughter in my head, or the lover
I didn't keep. Wicked stepmother,
the judge in court. At cocktail parties
I played the exile, didn't wear my jewels,
lost them, ignored my children,
dwelled on tribulation,
rewound it, made them play it over.

I was the orphan Seeta. And the mother of.
That is over. I am tired.
I think, sunshine on ships
when I travelled, laughs on Malabar Hill—
my life did not comprise me it was so brief.

65

Boucheron, Shalimar, More Shoes

Friday I get paid   checks for debt
cosmetics   Christmas bounty   I never
expect to see anyone I know
or I do if someone's widow stops me
it's as if I never saw her see me lost
in the mall looking for clearances
and for him I haven't seen   twenty
years or it seems like more   William
from Richmond got his father's lumber trust
this year stocks dropped London Bridge
all gone down blood pressure rising
who missed her mammogram?
I'm glad my job's with women
down in the Rayburn laws still passing
in low-heeled shoes red suits

I'll call AmVets to haul the attic loot
children you have from King's Birthday to
the Fourth to get yours out I'll give
the old *Britannica* to my carpenter's son
Great Books of the West save for the grand-
children's holidays how to divide the Annals
of America five ways? I get too many catalogs
I dream of trees   how did I manage
sidewalk grates stiletto nights?   the second
mortgage comes and William's greeting card
goes into the I'll-get-around-to-it basket
muffins Life coffee butter plums

William's divorced   the mail stops
time beyond the last tossed
wedding bouquets planted this future

Daughter-Mother-Maya-Seeta

To replay errors
the revolving door of days
Now it's over
There's no one point thank god in the turning world
I was always moving
tired too but laughing
To be a widow is an old
freedom I have known
Vidua paradisea   a bird
Singly I flew
and happiness was my giraffe
in the face of Africa
me among daughters
and my son at work
me pregnant with them
taking in the glamour days
town and country mirabella elle vogue
cosmopolitan   We have made this world
brown women
laughing till we cleared the dining table
In hotels men asked my girls to fetch them towels
In restaurants they asked us for bread
Today I'm a civil servant on the Hill

From the mall what colorful sarongs
my children bring to drape my ankles
the gifts we give

to Mina   pearls
Tara a Paloma purse for cosmetics
Lata a pair of lime shoes for the miles
Devi gives me her eclectic lit eyes
the glamour of our wilder regions
Bombay weavers on the twenty-four-hour looms
shocking pink is the navy of India

Listen I am listening
my mind is a trip
I took its English ships
I flew over oceans
I flew in the face of skies
orienting my loss of caste in a molting nation
my dark complexion
the folly of envy
wishing all my life to be fair
My jealous god leaves
Hello son this is your mother
Here daughters take these maroon saris
these maroon bras
I am proud to have borne you
When you gather around me
newness comes into the world

It's Me, I'm Not Home

Our person is a covered entrance to infinity
choked with the tatters of tradition

MINA LOY

At the Society for the Promotion of Indian Classical Music and Culture among Youth

Maestro plays a raga at dusk
which means God is great,
and we have our misery. It's true,
though downtrodden, we talk to God.

Maestro plays a raga at dusk which means
groceries are on stage (symbolism for starving people).
It's true, though downtrodden, we talk to him
(Thank you for onions and cabbage). But why

groceries on stage? Symbolism for starving people.
What will white people think of us? Corruption, poverty,
thank you for onions and cabbage. But why
must the singer make sure the lament goes on?

What will white people think of us?
Everyone feels devastated by the separation from God.
The singer makes sure the lament goes on
three hours. Happy New Year, it's the twenty-first century

separated from God.
Did my boyfriend sleep with you?
Happy New Year, it's the twenty-first century,
a moaning raga about the restless and

my boyfriend slept with you.
Visitors (all white) walk out

on the roaring raga about the jet set and
the distribution of oil, gold, crack, cars,

news they can't face, all white they walk out
on the Society for Indian Classical Music...
oil, gold, crack, cars, a world in which
we're miserable. Isn't God great?

It's Me, I'm Not Home

It's late in the city and I'm asleep.
You will call again? Did I hear
(please leave a message after the beep)

Chekhov? A loves B. I clap
for joy. B loves C. C won't answer.
In the city it's late, I'm asleep,

and if your face nears me like a familiar map
of homelessness: old world, new hemisphere
(it's me leave a message after the beep),

then romance flies in the final lap
of the relay, I pass the baton you disappear
into the city, it's late and I'm asleep

with marriages again, they tend to drop
by, faithful to us for about a year,
leave a message after the beep,

I'll leave a key for you, play the tape
when you come in, or pick up the receiver.
It's late in the city and I'm asleep.
Please leave a message after the beep.

What to Look for in a Man

When infatuations buried me,
I searched for glamour or some rich
element of his speech — the *je ne sais quoi*
of finesse, wit, strength, and drop-dead good looks.
I loved his job or another's clothes or the way
another ordered wine off a menu.
Pouilly-Fuissé I could not say at one time,
but once I could all men I dated had to have it right
or else. At home in his foreign accent, I eased
into the night's arms, forgot my language.
What was that? Hindi, Sindhi, Bengali, Punjabi.
Stranger eyes pierced me: *If you get here,*
I'll feed you. I got there, he fed me.
Love was touch and go if he didn't fit his coat,
if he sold his house, stopped going out, or lost
his money. What did I know?
All the things that make girls,
so when you spotted one you would say,
She is shallow, the brain of a bird.

A Winter Afternoon

What god freezes our lighted fountain
on winter afternoons? He's jealous we have fun.

No laughs, Amir's gone mad for Shaiyla. I say
to him, *What can I do? I'm not your woman.*

Waiting slenderizes me beyond the line of a
trace moon. Wonderfully rigid diet, San-

skrit clichés. Hearing me spar with my cousin,
breathless my husband picks up his phone.

I eavesdrop wildly in airports, not malls
only. I woo a counterfeit urban khan

to divorce. I send him trifles I adore.
Too busy to notice yes he talks shop on and on.

Granted I liked a certain drink, society pages.
What's he to me now, raw ambition.

Come on, Rekha, ease up, you convince me
this much is true, untrue, how you pine.

When I Was a Housewife

Give me a second to get caught up with fashion.
When seasons change, nothing does, only the way

I dress. That heartthrob belongs to his admirers.
Even I travel miles on the unreliable subway

to see him. He lauds my husband in public. Later
he saunters over, I'm unhappy, he wants me, I say okay.

My house comes together — sofas,
plants, drapes, his dare I should run away.

Don't bite my lip, he'll trace my smarting blades,
welts, imprints, kisses, he'll indict you on hearsay.

Give me one minute I live it up. Says in ancient texts
lack of love murdered whole tribes in a day.

I'm typical, a girl. They tell me I adore
love's battery. That's crazy. Didn't I court delay?

Life, Rekha, the laser-beam jungle we live in...
afternoons fly like a Saturday.

No Complaints

Poverty, what do I plan to do?
Sort my worn clothes and get rid
of silks dyed to match chapel blooms.
I want to discard the apparel of off-days,
so in the end I will have no complaints.
I want the phone to stop ringing,
though I am curious who calls.
I want to clear my head of errands,
auto inspection and passport renewal,
and travel with my love,
small sacks, and lottery money.
I want to walk the far hill and valley
and wrap a tropic on the short spit of my street,
and the nightclubs thrumming out
a tabla's bass roll in American tunes,
reckless longing at the first sight of land,
me and you, tall stranger
from the coffee stand, dark hand on my dark head
among the lit faces at bars,
shoulders like drums rimming a countertop world,
the quietly looped wife,
bartender turning and turning like a moon...
I want to scan all the frayed coasts
and mill through a Carnival's ports of Spain.
Where is that country nearest my blood?
Ink: it's on my hands.

Type A

Blind date is how I lucked out with him
doting on me in his heated Alfa Romeo
on the way to the developers' party
network for local business owners,
where I heard *right place at the right time*,
either that or a recording of it on-site.

Stock prices Mister Money recites
were a lure, but I loved his car more, so his
passion for deals all the time —
Trump to Turner to Fox, Romeo
to Juliet — was a trade-off. He owned
Hot Tomatoes and led the party

chatter. Showing up at a cocktail party
meant he'd cost-benefit you on sight,
count seats, turn tables, or why be an owner,
swim or you're done for. Did I choose him
or did he ensnare me pointing out a Romeo
Gigli dress I'd look good in? Great, what time

could we go get it? Mister, take a time-
out, let's travel. No, we just partied
with cigarettes, sang in his Alfa Romeo,
flipped the dial, parked to recite
the script: *Sweetheart, give me a light*. But his
potential as a restaurant owner

got me. I loved his flair as if I owned
his shoes, key ring, collar, no tie.
You felt done in by what you adored — his
Henry Kissinger–cool voice of the party,
American heiresses by his side,
sunroof down, seats all leather, this Romeo

drives circles around you with his Romeo-
mobile, he shifts gears like the owner
of the world's biggest construction site
in Saudi or the Sultan of Brunei for a time
in your head, it's incredible to party
as you do. Think of it: to take him

or leave him means the Alfa Romeo
party loop, his hands the way he owned
the right place the time he was out of sight.

Lullaby

I would not sing you to sleep.
I would press my lips to your ear
and hope the terror in my heart stirs you.

Beijing

Mao wanted to get rid of birds
because of the droppings;
then bugs took over and ate trees.
You leave the Forbidden City
single file, but the earth is so loose
it whirls at the gates. It is everywhere.
Trees are the only way to tame it.
Meanwhile where are they, dogs and cats?
Dust rises and storms around you.
No birds but bats. The earth
is solitary and uncontrolled;
a watery eye is its only home.

A Holiday at Home

Thanks to this century of travel,
I landed in the South, in this uninsulated
nineteenth-century house
I love, wrong side of the tracks,
but what a view of the train (forward
to Spain, I'm going to go),
and stringy town lights framed in asphalt.
I run on these streets thinking
it's fantastic out here on my own
singing a country hit tune,
truck's broke, dog's dead, but I'm singing.
Of all the voices this year
I love Machado's the most.
Poorly dressed, sad, and heavy,
he said, *O light-struck evening.*

Confederate

he doesn't look like a Citadel Cadet
no crew cut looks at me   nudges my arm
in Comp   *want a hamburger?*
I say, *since when do Hindus eat them*
you a Hindoo?   we pass

the English novel class his sister Faye
winks   won't tell Dad Jack
I ask him *what*   he says *to be*
Lakshmi Meera Narayan with him
means going undercover in his Jeep

I look for decals on his dashboard
anything to steer me no
sign   we order lunch
got it   he opens his wallet
gunning the engine he mentions a bed

and breakfast   what?   he drives
to the Rose Garden taupe walls pink
fabric softener tassels   cameos
no Reb flags hidden in his britches
a personal ad says *gay white male*

offering free weekend to active
duty guys no fats or fems
I've always dated white men   why no

New Delhi prep school boys?   no Chinese
no African   'cause doing it with him

I'm neon he's my peroxide
shelling out sixty-five to the owner
is this Bombay's red-light zone or
Patpong he's German self-exiled I'm
the Asian trump card up his sleeve

what does it mean? I can't find
the emblem   a bottle of Calvin Klein
rolls out from under the seat   back to
campus   Kali and Ray stenciled
in cement at Papa Jazz's sidewalk sale

he loses me for a white girl up ahead
déjà vu like something tattooed
on his shoulder I must've seen
my skin blues under fluorescent
catcalls I can't tell my father about

men I date can't tell the difference
between Jack and Jake until it's me
making sure my lipstick's on and then
he's gone   a vanishing point
on my face never turned me porcelain

Personal Ads

So I paid her twice a week
a lot of money to say
I picked the set
his pale hotel room he designed
to hide out with someone younger
than his wife   to ejaculate the wilddog
affection for the Dow Jones who knows
why I kept listening

       good girls clean the house your father will
said dear mother also known as the Mrs.
Apple falls close to the tree
I picked she picked
men whose promises

       running late sorry doll now I have to fly
       why don't you watch TV   here click
       or phone me in Dubai or leave
       a message with my secretary Darlene DeBeers
       all circuits busy please call back
       I'm in town only tonight
       I can't hear you
       know how loud's a freight train
       Do it

No I never said what I
girl's education never to displease
except I paid up twice a week to free me from
swallowing poison
jumping on tracks

having nothing for divorce   I owe
thirty-two thousand in filing fees
your honor thank you so much now I know
I slip on the rice-strewn steps
the steeple's staring
I'm no anchor
life's points will cut you
from packages at the mall
you will never overcome credit cards
never eat cake at your birthday party
children you never had will ask you why

Nikos of Caravy Street

Nikos, she said, don't kill yourself.
Or what will I tell your father?
He will beat me like he beat Ansey,
take my blue organdy dress,
he will raise up my mourning like a kite
above town, and he will work me,
tell me again how he likes his crabs,
cooked in salted butter. What a bore!
Give it some thought, Nikos.
You were always the selfish one
hogging the tailor's time at Easter,
bribing the butcher for your cut.
What about Nisseem?
What piece of mutton did he ever get?

So tell me Nikos,
are you coming to Andrade's for dinner,
or what shall I say?
Ah, he didn't feel up to it—
it is too hot for him to put on a shirt.

Ah Nikos, you are a bum!
Now get up. Get up before I tell your mother
and she comes rushing in here with her broom.

Get up, I am turning the iron up to silk—
give me your shirt, take off those trousers so I can crease them.
Who ever heard of a man lying around

in his best evening trousers?
These you put on for someone else's funeral—
Tarik's, for example. Now Tarik deserves to shoot himself.
Yesterday he seduced Laleh—
tomorrow Angelina.
Get up Nikos, don't think Tarik hasn't winked at me.
He calls here you know.
He calls and asks, *So
is Nikos dead? Has the poor creature cut his throat?*

Who cares for you Nikos de Mecina?
One minute left for dead,
the next putting on aftershave.

Nikos at 42

Today's like yesterday.
My wife tells me I'm sick;
it's true, she says I'm sick of life.
Sonia's the expert, knows everyone's
business on Caravy Street.

What's the use?
I lie on the bed
till 4:30 in the afternoon.
When she returns, she'll say,
Trinidad doesn't need more men like you!
The whole street offers her consolation.
She can go to her mother's anytime.
She has many aunts, too many:
hear them rail at my faults (pauper,
earns no money).

Some days I think, This day is like all others.
I take my hat and go out.
I buy bread.
I eat it on the way to the cigarette stand.
I light up and then I may talk to Emil,
metaphysical Emil full to the brim.
Long after my cigarette's out, I'm waiting.
Emil, my day demands, I say.
But he wants to talk about God. Yes,
I say I believe on occasions, sometimes I disbelieve.
He brightens — he thinks I'm complex after all.

At last I say, *Emil I got to go.*
The hurt look on his face, fine,
but I carry his sigh within my sigh.
I tell you it's no good.

Friend, I used to say, my street is full of kooks
flipping the white placard: OPEN, CLOSED
FOR LUNCH. In the past, how was I different?
As for women, there are names I can't shake off.
The beautiful Althea with the cinnamon tongue;
after Althea, Maura.
Women I loved, women who later clouded my name.
Now I don't even whore but my old ways follow me like a dog.

No bread, no more cigarettes.
Just me and the overeager birds.
What's it with them, clacking gossips
on the hill past Father Malgre's church?
The old people say, *Nikos go to the South Pole—*
you need to look at ice.
Why's the remedy always clear across the world?
Like when I'm thinking of Alvaro,
need to talk to Alvaro, but he's a waiter in Belgium.
Not only that, he's in a town I'll never find.
So what should I do? Wait all my life for the train?

I'll live to be eighty, I'll be ninety
like those would-be Braganzas in my line.
Shopkeepers, they pinned our name to a rented door,
and lasted a century each.
Sonia who doesn't listen always rushes out
for a better tablecloth.
If coffee dips to the last bean,

she runs to Coelho's store. Maybe that's the trouble.
Maybe I should say to her, *Relax, unbraid your hair.*
And Emil? what's his trouble anyway? —
he's begrudges normal conversation.

Little by little, I'll figure it out.
I'll say to them, *Relax, we'll live to be a hundred.*
If I sleep until dinner, what's lost?
I'll sort things out.
Then I'll go back to my job sorting mail.
Two, three hours pass away.

I've cleared out boredom, that dirty straw.
I'll look in the paper.
I'll live a long life.
We'll give a dinner party.
If Emil finds out, we'll invite Emil,
and all those who are sore at me, we'll take the quick
embrace by the door.

To Angelina from Nikos in His Old Age

The time comes, Angelina, and the day's blinking.
No sleeping around, no mother,
nothing interesting about the weather.
We played hooky a lot and made gossip.
But I thought you liked it, cheating on Nisseem
who became emperor of coffee —
      how'd he do it!
He was loaded, I was good in bed.
You got your rich husband,
and for years my cock.
You fussed over the time I
sprayed your new lilac dress twice in a row.
I loved your thick hair shaking
at the sink as you rinsed your dress.
My husband, you screeched,
      he will kill me he will sniff this he
      will chase me out with the dog!

Boy was I a nut.
You at thirty, I forty-five,
and Sonia my wife. If she caught the slightest cold,
      they said, *You poor angelic sufferer,*
      that lousy rat Nikos slept with gorgeous whores.
Pow pow what a lawsuit.
Come on, Lina, we have cheering up to do.
Do the calculus. I'm eighty, you're a luscious sixty-five,
      church pillar,
voluptuous benefactor you are practically the Pope.

You think I'll stain your reputation.
       Lina little closer I want to breathe you.

You're gray? So'm I,
       nobody's looking.
This is Trinidad. We were the left margin of Spain.
It is evening and I have no money.

Once I was great and you wanted me.
I surrender; I wanted you more.

Nevermind Althea, nevermind Lucky
from Kuala Lumpur,
and the Americans were just a lark, topless—
what could I do?

You were a woman. Forgive me I didn't tell you,
you were my spark, your low-cut bodice.
Don't rant at me later if I wink at you in church.
I, a Portuguese, wanted to claim Cervantes,
so all my life I rode my horse.

Laleh of Caravy Street

The way I dress, men think
many have me. They hoot
and drink. At parties I roll my eyes.

Though I'm twenty my mother says,
Do what I did Laleh get a man I'll give
you the flat I'll buy you china.

I'm off, Ma. Yes I was born here,
back of my father's building, two blocks
of Trinidad above Nisseem's shop,

the city, an island, southern, we've been,
we are. Now what? Ship relics.
If we stole gold back then, is that

nothing to me? I need a visa, ticket
out, black dress, luggage for shoes.

Letter to the Moor

How could I not see you
in my father's house evenings
you came for dinner and to talk
about wars. I loved heroics.
            But don't you know
            they are mine, too.
If I speak of this bluntly

they'll call me Bianca's twin, drunk
on cheap infatuation, a whore.
I have no words to limn interior
            climates. Nights. My arm
            clutches your dark brightness—
your arm on my paler one.

What are these skins if not ourselves?
One husband, one wife; that is how I see
our marriage. But we say
            moons need pitch to be seen.
            Midnight needs the moon
to stitch its cloak of wonders.

Living. What combinations.
Two skins and one per citizen. In books
black is beast. I'm Mary, alabaster,
            I'm the virgin dewlike
            morning flush. A flat world
but I roamed it hungrily.

From limb to limb I climbed men
in my mind, suitor after
suitor, next in line for Brabantio's
        daughter: men smiled: we
      talked of our childhoods
   in Venice. *I felt nothing.*

So let them call me a whore, say I deceived,
call you pornographic. Who conquered
whom, and what's the war now?
        A wolf's wish for days—
      for this hunger to keep
   alighting and your grip

to catch my skin's stark shattering.
Break my fall, I give it all up to you.
And if I wished heaven
        made me a man,
      I take back the words.
   I've given everything

to keep me as I am. Go
now—I'll keep missing you
like strong weather. I have your handkerchief
        of strawberries. I won't cry.
      Fierce holds have their ways.
   I'll outlast the ancient,

jealous disapprovals. What bred them?
I'll wait out storms and floods and flight
delays. I have one wish, Othello.
        Call it what you will,
      I call it a life.

Remembering Jean Rhys

To think of bitter memories back in one's sleep,
to catch rudeness from her flawless skin,
to bow to a banker.

Better to ride over to that boutique
for the dress and lipstick you've been waiting for,
better to wear them
and remember days you spoke with those you loved.
The lawyer who left you shillings for heat.
The art dealer–husband who showed you style,
got locked up for embezzling.
Sometimes money was easy.
Failure was not.
There you were by a hotel room's heater,
writing, rouged and ready, dressed to the nines.

Hamlet out in the Night

No one to talk to: no one,
and the word tunnels through me like a worm.
I love Horatio, but what can he know?
You clipped me from the collegiate moment,
happiness, my nation. So, Mother,
I go houseless into the street.
Moon, be wool for an army when I row
miles of cold lake in my shadow.
What's more beleaguering than water rippling
like a thousand frowns? There are no words,
only the exit, the catch
of her dress through a doorway
and an all-night feast of numbered stars.
One, two—I am
the electric insomniac—Christ I fizzle—
lights won't come on,
the seating looks wrong. Hurry
the boys to my skit.
I'm dying to talk. One week is a life.
I'll be in the street with my riddle.

From the Postcard at Vertigo Books in D.C.

In the photo of Billie Holiday at the 1957 Newport Jazz Festival, she wears a low-cut evening gown and fawn-colored stole. Her rhinestone earrings are shoulder-dusters, and her necklace falls almost to her cleavage in leaves of glass stones, or maybe they are real. The bracelet on her wrist spans wide as a man's shirt cuff, and her nails are frosted. The cigarette comes out at you, foreshortened over a score where notes are few with wide spaces between... Her hairline is even as Nefertiti's, eyebrows painted on with confidence, and her lips, most likely red, are round in generous laughter for the photographer. She is not singing: that was before, or she's going on later. Billie is chic on her break; and when women open little drawers of half-used lipsticks two shades off, and mascaras bought in anticipation, they know as I do looking at my stash of glamour—we look for it and it's not there.

Emigration

1

No packing list, and no money.
But I want the gold tasseled chaise

I lounged on those nights of havoc
speaking with you at 36 avenue Georges Mandel,

Maria Callas, about a heart's dryness,
a loss of verve, deeps of talent, glamour

not plumbed. Wanting Onassis even when strewn
scales were your fleet. Voluptuous. Rough.

I want a recording of that Medea.
I mean, Maria, your love for Jason.

Cravings. Radha wandering with love for Krishna.
A cowherding girl, penniless, electric.

2

Duvet cover, lamp, world, biography of Auden;
thing was to love one's neighbor... I strayed

to planes, trains, you, clothes.
Weren't they a carapace for fragile conversations?

I meant to call you but lost myself at the mall.
Friday at noon, the weekend, driving fast, not speaking,

tube of Aim, boarding pass, *Elle,*
the handbag of maps. Radha,

did I ever mail you my best greetings
from climates which hinted at something fine?

3

We wore cigarette-leg pants in melon silks
at the dress store, took breaks

in the stockroom and talked cosmetics,
made extravagant wishes to forgo

at these religious times — but even now I'd like
bronze mica frost with a dark brown liner.

I'll bring you Jean Rhys. What shade of rouge?
Tia, from the shoe store, size-two petite jacket,

you come too. And you, Anisa, always window-
shopping your mind, bring your steamer trunk

as if it were old days on a Cunard Line,
and made bold by emigration we wave from the rail.

4

Late dinners at Brasa off the downtown mall
where we keep on eating mussels

and talking about the day, *and did I say
I played it like a wild card?* — each shell

wet on our fingers, tossed off at the coast
where we go for the tide. Bye sailor. See you

Maria. What's to take? Maybe the sand
collecting her wet skirts on my chaise. Hello

beach and weather. Good morning
passport checkpoint, the lighted coast.

No Sabotage

The soul goes in search of omega
on the lips of other grails.
Books paint trouble, heiress, seductress,
Karenina, Bovary, *The House of Mirth*.
You regret mossy gifts you did not keep,
virgin myth you almost believed,
wake up with the wardrobe of the scorned
on her last night. That's not your faille
dress's white lie dropped at a dinner.
Holidays are not the horn-tooting family.
Instead, no peers but fast avenues
rimming your high building, slate
sky vast as a head, and the sea.
Unconquered, not conquering, you go,
spent, elated you are on the road.

Letter from Blacksburg

Boston's teeming streets.
George, I have come to the mountains
and remember how we walked along Winthrop's coast
that summer wet with heat.
By October, fall froze us, and you strode on,
modern Greek and village songs. Christmas
at a restaurant we saw a belly dancer and thought of home.

I left for Georgia, and after Georgia,
Virginia, until I had moved five times.
You stayed on your rocky shore.
In this town sprawling with bright jackets,
and buildings flat and tan with local stone,
I stare into cold air hard as a lip in this wind.
I took some turns on Southern roads.
It's winter, bracing limbs for new days.

You write, we'll meet at the Greek restaurant.
Those Greeks, always dreaming of summer.
We looked at travel posters—sun and sky—
and when they turned up the heat we called it nostalgia.
In booths we burned in January.
We froze on the streets. You talked
of Cleopatra's sons. What could I say?
Aurangabad, Jaisalmer. Did I know
a few names and a local script? We walked,
and you, misquoting Jarrell, would say,

The saris go by us from the embassies.
We felt the comfort of cloth, an aunt's paisley arm
as if the soil were new to us.

For days, nothing but bright hours.
Noon and the sun blinds me.
Looking back, it is two months divided by rain.
I remember you lit with learning,
walking with the islander, he with sun
up his sleeve, sea ambling in his throat;
and if, in Boston, he walked as through Castries,
then you were in Greece, and I rode on Marine Drive
in Bombay. We had come far to have never left.

I had hoped for an angel to meet me
with another life — to be a planet,
purple, conversing with luminaries.
Those days I loved Icarus.
Years, we are grown.
I turn to come home again,
Main Street, Washington, Clay.
The air is thin. Skin dries.
And Constantin, *the talks we had,*
talks we are having.

Self and Soul Take Two

My hair was black as night sea.
              I always wanted platinum
blonde, but it washed out in one week.

I had eyes clear as paper. They're red
            from reading my green card
brochure. My ears led me

to love's whisper. Wonderful,
            he was leading me on,
and I let him. I had a girl's voice.

            I chain-smoked to get it deep as
        Garbo's. I had the eight arms
of a lover; I'm back to two;

and my legs which once wrapped you:
            I wouldn't mind it again,
                walking cities at festival hours.

I practiced religions, all are good,
            time-consuming and a chore. My dresses
enough for a line of wedding friends, but now I want

         even more, elegant, useless on display—I keep
changing my mind—I had a house
            in my name and a red door to the house.

To Imran in Bombay

Salaam aleikhem, Imran, once more
the time has come to be cured,
to toss out love letters and canceled stamps.
I'm back, and in Bombay I ate mangoes
on your stainless-steel plates. Malik and you
shook my arm and said, *Challo, let's go.*

In my car, mile markers flash,
and you vanish. The radio's music
swallows pavement, I'm open, a road.
Five years back, I said, *It's been five years.*
Now at ten, where's the morning?

At the post office, a Chinese boy
buys an aerogram. His grandmother takes it,
pastel paper, blue meandering veins,
your wild signature. The warm day
invades, I get back in my car.
Next to my arm evening falls, and I am still driving
in circles, past India Gate, India Gate.
Smells of fish and salt, smells of piss and dirt,
a zoo in my nostrils.
When we chatted over samosas, you said,
Stick with India, as if it were a drink,
our hands under the table like a bribe.

Bombay's purple hazes my mind, the red
of your wedding, crowds at the feast

dished out on the city's rice,
tents over grass, and the parade
of golden saris wishing you four stages:
knowledge, children and wealth,
wisdom, then faith's slow cast off.

Hindus say they crave wisdom but
wealth comes first, and
distance is an affectionate latitude.
My street splits the equator. Farewell
Imran, sneaking around, our blood pressure's high,
gods, holidays, relatives, duty-free shops.
Halfway, meet me, Athens, Rome, Frankfurt.
For blown kisses look to the stars,
the eyes of planes, the lights of travelers.

Dolmen Builder

If you don't live it, it won't come out of your horn.

CHARLIE PARKER

In a studio the smell of glue
Two long leaves for feet you scuffle
like early fall   play Ellington   Basie   Monk
all day build models of those giant loners
scaled to inhabit a city block   corner or park
Terse
       god knows what you sculpt in your mind
Sometimes after dark or first thing in the morning
over Coleman Hawkins and coffee
lingering like heat burns off a dolmen
raised by men but who knows   we get together
Backdrop   marks on a sundial   it's ticking
fast-forwarding to your breath on my back—
       it is so good to see you
       working on wooden models for the huge
       improvisations in a few chords on the scale
       of prairies   lost runes   mark
       of a race   some rare encounter   awestruck
       you get up   but is there no one to watch?
       It went so far into the future   a pure presence
       larger than its shape   huge lark of a man
       or facts from a past you tap the strange edges

Shuffle

Foolscap the shape of whys
No jazz on Seventh Avenue last
night of '99   I was
a hairpin turn on my mother's
map eyeing the world of you
from the bottom of my cup
I ate dal and mangoes laid
postcards in my arms because I
don't sleep hard   Hawk's sax
held my breath   Rubber stamps
inked visas   Hordes changed nations
blew their minds   I lost one
to suicide   your four daughters
went to war   We hadn't met

I wasn't born   abroad you left
grade school waved like a prince
thirty-five years though darling
I couldn't see you over white
water   Parentheses who removed
Pacific? Atlantic?   I migrated
The IRS took your time
I lapsed in my single mother
you flashed back wired on wine
grandfathers braced us   I got
cancer you got brave   what a
gambit   You said, *Buddy can you*
Yeah when you least expect
a third set   co-incident call and

response   *Will you have me?*
The album started up again
Most definitely yes I will
many moons   Who's counting
Days without you tick inchingly
Vacations fly   Clock face's
handmade march steps around
the corner of a limb I adore
shapes of my near-miss   Time's not
decks do riffle luck of the   You
said *Draw cut and deal brown eyes*
my yard opens come in to be flesh
again your forehead is a flight
pad for my copter   These gifts

unwrap and render me   I thank
Grandmother said *Think twice about*
liquor we made this tribe soberly
in a wink we still happen in you
young one wet in my womb thinking

Dedicated to You

It is the thing you do   open a book
by someone you like who never knew you
you leaf through to see
which words are dedicated to you
What gives you this posthumous feeling
Well   you like his work and want your name in it
like on his dance card when there were
evening dances at your grandfather's supper club
You see Miguel Hernández and Mirabai
Dickinson Ghalib and Hayden
Carlos "Don't Kill Yourself" Drummond de Andrade
but not you   you wonder when you will appear
This is more than the desire to see you engraved
in stone as an original donor to the Morgan Library
or listed in your alumnae magazine
Charter Member of the President's Circle
This is the affair you had
dedication is only part of the proof
the rest is hand-canceled
stashed in a box made of sandalwood
lined with department-store tissue
the rain presses you to find
you are there in the pantheon
You knew it
this poet born in England died in 1950
after India's Independence
when murder was breakfast cereal and people hoarded fists
your grandfather divorced your grandmother

who went for a Muslim in Bombay
no more dances at that house of cards
Therefore your mother an only child gave birth to orphans
D.C.   the fifty states   and Puerto Rico
You fly across the world like mail in 1968
in the bright days of war
and department-store parades
This poet loves her readers
and you loved him who died before you were born

It's a Young Country

and we cannot bear to grow old
James Baldwin   Marilyn Monroe
Marvin Gaye sing the anthem
at the next Superbowl
We say *America you are*
magnificent   and we mean
we are heartbroken
What fun we chase after it
Can't hurry go the Supremes
Next that diva soprano
for whom stagehands at the Met
wore the T-shirt *I Survived the Battle*

We leave for a better job
cross the frontier   *wish you*
were here in this hotel   Two of us one
we are with John Keats on his cot
in the lone dictionary I'm falling
on dilemma's two horns
If you are seducing another
teach me to share you with humor
Water in my bones and the sound
of a midnight telephone   *Hello love*
I am coming   I do not know
where you sleep   are you alone

We grow old   look at this
country its worn dungarees
picking cotton dredging ditches
stealing timber bullets prairies
America's hard work have mercy
in order to form a more perfect
some step forward some step back
neighbor here's a seat at my table
through orange portals lit tunnels
over bridges Brooklyn Golden Gate
weather be bright wheels turn yes
pack lightly we move so fast

About the Author

Reetika Vazirani is the author of *White Elephants* (Beacon Press, 1996), which won a Barnard New Women Poets Prize. She is a recipient of a Pushcart Prize, a *Poets & Writers* Exchange Program Award, the Glenna Luschei Award from *Prairie Schooner*, a "Discovery"/*The Nation* Award, and a Thomas J. Watson Fellowship. Born in India in 1962, she is a graduate of Wellesley College. She received her M.F.A. from the University of Virginia, where she was a Henry Hoyns Fellow. She is currently the Writer-in-Residence at the College of William & Mary.

Notes and Dedications

The quote from Louise Bogan on page vii is from "Women."

"Boarding: Independence": for Vijay Prashad.

"Tiffin for Tea, Lorry for Truck": the Woolf quote is from "The Mark on the Wall."

"It's Raining": for Robin Becker and Greta Niu.

"Maharaja of Patiala": for Jane and Stanley Moss. The Pessoa quote is from "Tobacco Shop," translated by Edwin Honig.

"Gina Lollobrigida": for Andrea Sirotti.

"Rahim Multani": the Howard quote is from "1915."

"Pandavas' Gamble": the Seferis quote is from "Our country is closed in," translated by Edmund Keeley and Philip Sherrard.

"Watching the News": for Pat Waters. The Villon quote is from "The Old Lady's Lament for Her Youth," translated by Robert Lowell.

"Letter to Jaipur": for Jennifer Brice and Jackye Pope. The Pasternak quote is from "For Anna Akmatova," translated by Robert Lowell.

"Seeta": the Berryman quote is from "#332."

"Daughter-Mother-Maya-Seeta": for Hilda Raz and Marilyn Nelson.

The quote from Mina Loy on page 71 is from "O Hell."

"Type A": for Peter Dissin.

"Letter to the Moor": for Richard Howard.

"Remembering Jean Rhys": for Diane Elaine Taylor.

120

"Emigration": for Rita Dove.

"Letter from Blacksburg": for George Kalogeris.

"Dolmen Builder": for Clement Meadmore. The Parker quote is from Carl Woideck's *Charlie Parker*.

The Chinese character for poetry is made up of two parts: "word" and "temple." It also serves as pressmark for Copper Canyon Press.

Founded in 1972, Copper Canyon Press remains dedicated to publishing poetry exclusively, from Nobel laureates to new and emerging authors. The Press thrives with the generous patronage of readers, writers, booksellers, librarians, teachers, students, and funders — everyone who shares the conviction that poetry invigorates the language and sharpens our appreciation of the world.

PUBLISHERS' CIRCLE

The Allen Foundation for the Arts
Lannan Foundation
National Endowment for the Arts

EDITORS' CIRCLE

Thatcher Bailey
The Breneman Jaech Foundation
Cynthia Hartwig and Tom Booster
Port Townsend Paper Company
Target Stores
Emily Warn and Daj Oberg
Washington State Arts Commission

The publication of this book is also made possible
with the generosity of LEF Foundation

For information and catalogs:

COPPER CANYON PRESS
Post Office Box 271
Port Townsend, Washington 98368
360/385-4925
www.coppercanyonpress.org

This book is set in the digital version of
Figural, designed by Oldřich Menhart in
1940 and redrawn for Letraset in 1992
by Michael Gills. Book design by Valerie
Brewster, Scribe Typography. Printed on
archival-quality Glatfelter Author's Text
by Malloy, Inc.